Seiyu Kiriyama, Founder (Kancho) of Agon Shu, sends out his message from New York to the rest of the world: True wisdom will open the way to our future.
(Unitarian Church of All Souls, New York, November 4, 2000)

Photographs by Kengo Tarumi

As Kiriyama Kancho begins fire meditation in front of the sacred flames the entire gathering prays together as one.

The *goma* fire ceremony in New York. The sacred fire arises, transmitting Buddhist truth and creating a sanctified space. (Unitarian Church, November 4, 2000)

The Unitarian Church, site of the New York *goma* ceremony and talk, has a proud 180-year history. Herman Melville, author of *Moby Dick,* was a member.

Guests inscribing their prayers on prayer sticks.

Kiriyama Kancho teaches that there are three guiding principles indispensable to the future of mankind: a conversation with one's soul, a battle with the mind, and the acquisition of wisdom. These principles are the objectives of Agon Buddhism and may be obtained through the Buddhist ritual known as the *goma* ceremony.

The Unitarian Church was filled to capacity with over 700 New Yorkers who listened attentively to Kiriyama Kancho's talk.

Agon Shu's *goma* ceremony marks a new historical moment in the life of the Unitarian Church, a meeting place for New York religious society.

THE WISDOM OF THE *GOMA* FIRE CEREMONY

THE WISDOM OF THE *GOMA* FIRE CEREMONY

by
Seiyu Kiriyama
Founder of Agon Shu Buddhist Association

Translated by Rande Brown

HIRAKAWA SHUPPAN INC.

Copyright © 2001 by Seiyu Kiriyama
All rights reserved.
No part of this publication may be reproduced
without prior permission in writing from the publisher.

First published in 2001 by HIRAKAWA SHUPPAN INC.
Mita 3-1-5, Minato-ku, Tokyo 108-0073, Japan

Japanese-English Translation by Rande Brown
In collaboration with
Michiko Abe and Fukiko Kai
Designed by Akihiko Tanimura
Printed and bound in Japan by
NISSHA Printing Co., Ltd.
Paper Supplied by Nakasho, Inc.

Translated from the Japanese original,
first published in 2001 by HIRAKAWA SHUPPAN INC.,
under the title *Nyuyoku yori sekai ni mukete hassinsu*.

Niebuhr,G.:
"For a Historic Church,One More milestone"
11/04/2000
Copyright © 2000 by the New York Times Co,
Reprinted by permission.

Contents

Sending Out a Message to the World from New York City ········7

On the Occasion of Agon Shu's *Goma* Fire Ritual in New York City: A Message from Seiyu Kiriyama, Founder of Agon Shu Buddhist Association ········8

Why New York? Why Now? ········11

New York Will Understand ········12

"You've Received a Request for a Newspaper Interview" ········14

"If One Grain of Wheat Abides" ········17

My Greatest Joy ········21

Standing at the Religious Crossroads of the World ········23

Sending Out a Message to the World from New York City ········24

Article from the *New York Times*
For a Historic Church, One More Milestone ········25

Text of New York Speech
A Conversation with One's Soul, A Battle with the Mind, and the Acquisition of Wisdom ········31

Towards Attaining semi-Nirvana ········47
  True Happiness Is Obtained through Wisdom ········48
  Establishment of a Training Center ········50
  Begin by Healing Mind and Body ········54
  Proper Nutrition Supports Spiritual Practice ········58
  Strengthening Mind and Body ········61
  Sakrdagamin: Intellectual Completion ········63

Sending Out a Message to the World from New York City

On the Occasion of Agon Shu's *Goma* Fire Ritual in New York City: A Message from Seiyu Kiriyama, Founder of Agon Shu Buddhist Association

I believe that the two most important things for the human race at the present time are for us to love our fellowmen without discrimination or bias and to attain a state of higher wisdom.

The fact that even now, at the beginning of the 21st century, the human race is still trapped in the turmoil caused by conflict, war and poverty is expressly due to the lack of these qualities. May I suggest that, in particular, the primary reason for this situation is our lack of higher wisdom?

It isn't that we lack sufficient love towards our fellow human beings. I believe that the human race already possesses the love and compassion that religion teaches us are necessary to our lives. I believe that we are born with these qualities.

So if we are by nature inherently loving and compassionate, then how do we explain the realities of hatred, murder, assault, and theft?

I believe these things continue to exist because we lack wisdom, not because we lack love and compassion.

Higher wisdom is what enables us to discover and awaken the love and compassion that are within us and to extend them properly to others. I believe that wisdom, like love and compassion, is inherent to our nature and is something that we need to value and to cherish.

This is not just my own personal opinion. It is something that was taught by the Buddha.

The esoteric fire ritual that we are going to hold in New York is a method of meditation based on the teachings of the Buddha that is designed to develop and elevate our wisdom to a higher plane.

In performing the *goma* fire ritual, I hope to focus attention on the wisdom contained within the Buddha's teachings and to spread awareness of the importance of attaining this wisdom for oneself.

I especially hope to have an impact on the young. If young people were as interested in attaining wisdom as they are in excelling at sports, the 21st century could witness the dawn of a marvelous new world. And I am confident that young people will be able to see that this particular form of meditation is, in fact, a wonderfully compelling intellectual sport.

New York is the information center of the world and the source of much of its news. I have long wanted to perform a *goma* fire ritual in New York City, and hope that as many people as possible will be able to partake in the experience. Nothing would make me happier than to share this experience with you. I thank you for your kindness and support.

July, 2000

Why New York?
Why Now?

Why did I send this message off to New York?

It's because, at this point in time, I felt that New York is where it absolutely had to go.

There are a number of reasons for this.

In the same way that the industrial revolution which started in the 18th century brought about profound changes in industrial productivity and social organization through the development of steam locomotion and electrical power, the recent developments in information technology foretell the beginning of yet more revolutionary changes in our history. Against the backdrop of remarkable innovations in electronic and communications technology, IT's field of application is expanding rapidly to instigate profound changes in areas as diverse as commerce, finance, governance, and social culture. We can't yet begin to see where it is all going to end.

Those who are not able to respond appropriately to these revolutionary changes are surely going to meet with failure and be left behind.

But I don't think an adequate response can come only in terms of technology. I believe that it has to come from the spirit as well.

The revolution in technology requires a corresponding revolution in spirituality.

We must take the outmoded spiritual system of the *ancien regime* and create a new paradigm for the future.

Arthur Koestler noted in his book *Janus* as early as 1978:

> The most striking indication of the pathology of our species is the contrast between its unique technological achievements and its equally unique incompetence in the conduct of its social affairs.

I don't agree with Koestler that our problems are caused by a "pathology of our species." I think the species has been so focused on the forward development of technology that we have been amiss in our application of wisdom.

Seventeen years have passed since Koestler committed suicide. Our "unique technological achievements" have come to surpass what even he could have imagined. Have we seen a corresponding increase in wisdom?

New York Will Understand

And how has the world spiritual community responded to the reality of the changes that are occurring?

It seems to me that its response has been very much behind the times. Profound changes have already occurred in the individual and in society, yet religion keeps delivering the same old spiritual messages, over and over again. Messages that encode doctrine that was formulated hundreds, even thousands, of years ago. I suggest that this may be one of the reasons for Koestler's observation that the species has been strikingly incompetent in the conduct of its social affairs.

I decided to try to blow a breath of fresh air into this stagnant situation.

As we move into the third phase of the technological revolution, I am determined to do what I can to spark a spiritual revolution.

As we stand on the brink of the 21st century our hearts and minds are filled with hopes and expectations about the developments that will occur in many spheres over the new century, including that of religion.

It would be terribly sad to think that there isn't a religious body in the world that is able to answer those expectations.

A new wind must blow! And I must be the one to try to do it!

This is the sentiment I was trying to communicate in the message that I sent off to New York.

Why didn't I choose Japan?

Because I thought that any wind which could move

the world had to emanate from its center.

I thought that New York would understand because it is an international gathering place for people of great intelligence and sensibility.

I decided this is where I would throw down my challenge.

This is where I would attempt to communicate, in this international center of excellence, New York.

I reasoned that if New York didn't understand what I was trying to communicate then neither would the rest of the world. And if New York wasn't able to understand, then I would accept my defeat with good grace. I would let New York and the rest of the world go, for now, assuming they were not ready to understand me. I felt confident in my decision and determined to do my best.

"You've Received a Request for a Newspaper Interview"

I arrived at John F. Kennedy Airport on November 2 at 10:30 in the morning.

A number of my staff members were pushing their way through the crowd to greet me. They immediately informed me that I had received a request for a newspaper interview.

I was surprised and asked, "Oh, which one?"

"The *New York Times*."

"What?" I stopped in my tracks. I thought maybe I had misheard. "Which newspaper?"

"The *New York Times*. What do you want us to do? They want to interview you at 1:30. That doesn't give you much time..."

"How long will it take us to get to the hotel?"

"It should take about 50 minutes."

"Then we have enough time. It's okay. Please tell them I agree to the interview."

As I was riding along in the car my jet lag and lack of sleep just flew out the window.

I couldn't believe it.

The *New York Times*, known world-wide for its sound judgement and excellent reputation, was asking me for an interview!

I had just put my feet down on American soil. I hadn't even done anything yet. Why did the *New York Times* want to interview me?

Then I nodded.

"Maybe it was the message," I said to myself.

Maybe someone picked up on the message I sent ahead.

"This really is New York," I thought. It is like I imagined. I had been perceiving things straight. Maybe the discriminating intelligentsia of New York would be interested in me.

I was very touched.

Of course, I realized that being interviewed didn't necessarily mean that there would be an article. And if there was an article, there was no guarantee that it would be positive. But still, at least, I knew that someone had paid attention to my heartfelt message.

I must say, though, that I was very impressed by the speed and timeliness of the response. "How like America," I thought.

When I arrived at the hotel I was told that there was another major newspaper which had also asked for an interview, but that one was scheduled for a few days later.

I had a light meal and was getting ready for the interview when I was told that it was going to be conducted over the phone.

People bustled about the hotel room checking the phone set-up.

The call came in at the appointed time.

Ms. Rande Brown, who translates my books into English, acted as interpreter.

I was told that Gustav Niebuhr was the name of the journalist who would be interviewing me and that he was the religion editor of the *New York Times*.

Even though it is only to be expected of someone in his position, I was surprised at the extent of Mr. Niebuhr's knowledge about Buddhism. He readily understood my answers to his questions. When I initially heard that the interview was going to be conducted by phone I was a bit concerned about how well we would be able to communicate, but my fears were unfounded. As the article shows, he clearly understood what I meant to say. I quote:

"In a written statement, he said the ritual 'is a method of meditation' intended 'to develop and elevate our wisdom to a higher plane.'"

His comprehension made me wonder if he had read any of my books. Now when people in English-speaking countries ask us about Agon Shu, we could almost hand over this article as a way of explanation.

The article further notes that "the attainment of this wisdom...awakens love and compassion," which is the point that I most wanted to stress. What a first-rate journalist.

The interview went on for over an hour.

The gratification of being able to express myself so thoroughly made me forget any weariness I might be feeling from my journey. Whether the interview was published or not, I was satisfied that I had done my best.

"If One Grain of Wheat Abides"

It was the morning of November 4, the day of the *goma* service and talk.

As soon as I arose I received a call from my secretary. An article had appeared that morning in the *New York Times*.

I never expected an article to appear on the very morning of the day of the event. I asked him to bring me a copy of the paper right away. I skimmed it quickly.

English is not my *forte*, so I wasn't able to understand all of it, but the first thing I noticed was that the article had a by-line. That usually lends weightier significance to the contents of the piece. Secondly, I saw that the article was longer than I thought it would be.

I understood enough to realize that the general tenor of the article was positive.

That meant that more people might well attend the event than we were expecting.

When we began to plan a *goma* ceremony for New York I imagined that we might attract 100 or so people. I hoped they would be serious, well-intentioned, thinking individuals. If 200 people happened to attend, and if they understood and responded to my message, then it would be a success. It would be a good start. Those 200 would become 2,000. Those 2,000 would become 20,000, and so on. I was sowing a seed. And this first gathering of people was like a single grain of wheat.

As the saying goes, "If one grain of wheat abides…"

We would cultivate this single grain with care.

One grain becomes a thousand grains, which become ten thousand grains, and before long there is enough bread to feed all the people in the world. That is what I thought.

But, needless to say, I also thought that if more people came that would be even better.

We were planning on broadcasting this event live to our 43 temples in Japan by satellite, and if the audience were sparse it wouldn't create a very good impression back at home. But now I started to worry that more people might show up than we would be able to accommodate. It was a pleasant worry to have.

And that's exactly what happened.

The sanctuary was filled to capacity.

The doors were scheduled to open at 4:00. People began to gather outside of the church before 2:00, eventually forming a long line. I started to realize that there might not be enough room for everyone.

As noted in the *New York Times* article, the Unitarian Church of All Souls is an elegant church with a long and distinguished history. Due to fire regulations, we were only permitted to allow 500 people to enter the main sanctuary.

But since I didn't expect more than a few hundred people to attend, I wasn't particularly concerned one way or the other. Then, starting about a month before the event, I was pleased to hear that our center in New York was receiving many inquiries about the event and requests for information. That's when we first began to suspect that we might have a full house.

I remember one request in particular. It came from a high school teacher who very much wanted to attend and wondered if it would be possible for him to bring 20 of his students to the event. I was touched by his interest and made sure he was told that he and his students were more than welcome.

My staff was beginning to worry that the hall wouldn't be large enough so they arranged with the church to set up video monitors in a communal room in the basement to handle any spillover. It was a good decision.

The seats in the main sanctuary filled quickly after the doors were opened. People jammed the aisles on either side of the hall. We were not allowed to admit any more people into the room and directed the extra guests downstairs to the temporary viewing space. But that soon filled up as well.

Finally, Ms. Gorycki, the church administrator, had to go outside and physically prevent more people from entering. She had to close the main doors.

In the end we had to turn away over 200 people. I imagine that some of these people had driven for hours to get there, and I felt so badly for them that it hurt.

I felt particularly bad about the high school teacher and his 20 students. There weren't enough seats for them so they had to go sit in the basement, and then, on top of that, there weren't enough earphones to go around so they couldn't hear the translation of the speech. I felt terrible about it and offer him my sincere apology. I will be sure that he receives priority seating the next time we hold an event here.

The fire ceremony and the talk were a big success. People stayed in the hall long after the event was over. They appeared to be enjoying the afterglow and looked like they didn't want to leave.

One compliment stands out from the many good wishes I received. The words "We New Yorkers have been hungry for this kind of spirituality for a long time" remain etched in my heart.

My Greatest Joy

On November 6 we hosted a social gathering that was attended by many distinguished New Yorkers.

The dinner took place at Brooklyn's River Café, which has magnificent nighttime views of Manhattan. As the name suggests, the restaurant is located on the banks of the Hudson River. It is a gracious and luxurious establishment.

The assembled guests represented a cross section of professions. There were artists, and lawyers, and architects.

I stood up and made the following speech:

> The recent *goma* ceremony and talk were an enormous success. I humbly offer my sincerest gratitude to all of you whose support and cooperation contributed to this achievement.
>
> Many joyful things have happened to me during this visit, but I would like to tell you about the one that has made me the happiest.
>
> It was the article so kindly published in the *New York Times*.
>
> The fact that this most prestigious and authoritative of journals printed an article about Agon Shu indicates to me nothing less than a certain level of acceptance in the West.
>
> The article gave me much encouragement. It added to my confidence and determination.
>
> And this encouragement, this confidence, and this courage will act to strengthen my efforts in the future.
>
> I hope that the tenets and ideas of Agon Shu will continue to be transmitted into the world from this locus of information, New York City.
>
> Thank you all for your support.

I received a stirring round of applause. This further increased my feelings of encouragement, confidence, around so they couldn't hear the translation of the speech. I felt terrible about it and offer him my sincere apology. I will be sure that he receives priority seating the next time we hold an event here.

The fire ceremony and the talk were a big success. People stayed in the hall long after the event was over. They appeared to be enjoying the afterglow and looked like they didn't want to leave.

One compliment stands out from the many good wishes I received. The words "We New Yorkers have been hungry for this kind of spirituality for a long time" remain etched in my heart.

My Greatest Joy

On November 6 we hosted a social gathering that was attended by many distinguished New Yorkers.

The dinner took place at Brooklyn's River Café, which has magnificent nighttime views of Manhattan. As the name suggests, the restaurant is located on the banks of the Hudson River. It is a gracious and luxurious establishment.

The assembled guests represented a cross section of professions. There were artists, and lawyers, and architects.

I stood up and made the following speech:

> The recent *goma* ceremony and talk were an enormous success. I humbly offer my sincerest gratitude to all of you whose support and cooperation contributed to this achievement.
>
> Many joyful things have happened to me during this visit, but I would like to tell you about the one that has made me the happiest.
>
> It was the article so kindly published in the *New York Times*.
>
> The fact that this most prestigious and authoritative of journals printed an article about Agon Shu indicates to me nothing less than a certain level of acceptance in the West.
>
> The article gave me much encouragement. It added to my confidence and determination.
>
> And this encouragement, this confidence, and this courage will act to strengthen my efforts in the future.
>
> I hope that the tenets and ideas of Agon Shu will continue to be transmitted into the world from this locus of information, New York City.
>
> Thank you all for your support.

I received a stirring round of applause. This further increased my feelings of encouragement, confidence, and determination.

Standing at the Religious Crossroads of the World

The pastor of the Unitarian Church, Rev. Forrester Church, was quoted in the article. I was deeply impressed by his words:

"In the 19th century, All Souls played a role as a 'religious crossroads' of New York... 'This is an opportunity for us to make it a religious crossroads for the world.'"

I was struck by the synchronicity of his remark. Here I was, attempting to blow a fresh religious wind into the world, and Rev. Church chose the expression "to make it a religious crossroads for the world."

It's like he was unwittingly giving me a hint about the road I need to follow.

"A religious crossroads for the world."

I continue to ponder the significance of these words.

Sending Out a Message to the World from New York City

In any event, it is interesting that when we began to plan this *goma* ceremony I declared, somewhat boastfully, that "I intend to send a message about Agon Buddhism from New York City, the information capital of the planet, out into the rest of the world." And, in the end, that is what happened.

I can say this because of the fact that the *New York Times* article that was published on Nov. 4 is now accessible through the newspaper's website on the internet. In this way, the information is now being made available to the world.

I am reminded of how extraordinary the power of faith and determination can be.

I am so grateful for the enthusiastic support of my followers and the many other people who helped make these events possible. I thank you from the bottom of my heart for the blessing of your cooperation.

We are at the beginning of a new path. I will not waver in my resolution to lead us down it.

Article from
the *New York Times*
November 4, 2000

For a Historic Church, One More Milestone
What's a goma? A big event where Melville prayed.
by
GUSTAV NIEBUHR

The Wisdom of the *Goma* Fire Ceremony

The Unitarian Church of All Souls, whose elegant building stands at the corner of 80th Street and Lexington Avenue in Manhattan, carries historic associations with such creative figures as Herman Melville, who was a member, and its onetime pastor the Rev. Henry Whitney Bellows, who built the United States Sanitary Commission to care for the sick and wounded of the Civil War.

But today the church will achieve another distinction, as the setting for a public prayer ceremony involving the kindling of a sacred fire by a Japanese Buddhist organization that has never before performed the rite in North America.

The ceremony, a *goma*, is a central rite of the Agon Shu Buddhist Association, which is based in Kyoto and was founded in 1978 by the Rev. Seiyu Kiriyama, its chief abbot. The ceremony is intended to "elevate the mind and the heart of the people in the audience," Mr. Kiriyama said through a translator in a telephone interview after arriving in New York on Thursday.

Mr. Kiriyama is 80 years old, the father of three grown daughters and the author of many Japanese-language books about Buddhist practice. As he described it, he founded his organization after a decades-long quest for a Buddhism that would lead practitioners directly to wisdom.

Worldwide, Buddhism exists in three major traditions: Mahayana, Theravada and Vajrayana.

Mahayana is predominant in Japan, China and Korea, and incorporates Zen Buddhism, the area of Japanese Buddhism probably most familiar to Americans. Mr. Kiriyama began his studies within the Mahayana tradition, but became dissatisfied and embarked on a search that led him to the Chinese translations of the scriptural texts (called sutras, in Sanskrit) that are central to Theravada Buddhism. That Buddhist tradition is dominant in Sri Lanka and Southeast Asia, and claims to adhere more strictly to the original practices established by the historical figure of the Buddha, who lived about 2,500 years ago.

It is from the agamas, four major collections of these texts, that the Agon Shu association derives part of its name. "Basically, there's only one group of sutras that the Buddha himself actually taught," Mr. Kiriyama said. "In the sutras that the Buddha taught, the agama sutras, there is the message for the acquisition of wisdom."

How the fire ritual facilitates the acquisition of wisdom is something Mr. Kiriyama said he would discuss at the event today. In a written statement, he said the ritual "is a method of meditation" intended "to develop and elevate our wisdom to a higher plane." The attainment of this wisdom, he said, awakens love and compassion.

The Wisdom of the *Goma* Fire Ceremony

The event, for which there is no charge, is to begin at 4:45 p.m. with music on flute and drum, followed by the kindling of the fire on an altar. Afterward, Mr. Kiriyama will deliver his talk, in which, he said, he will also discuss how the ritual differs from other fire ceremonies, in Buddhism and other predominantly Asian religions.

Mr. Kiriyama's association operates 64 temples in Japan, and counts 35 ordained priests and 400,000 members there. It also lists a number of philanthropic and educational efforts in various nations, including aid for earthquake victims in Turkey and scholarships in China and Mongolia. The money, Mr. Kiriyama said, comes from the association's members, who pay dues of $20 a month.

In recent decades, new religious and spiritual movements have proliferated in East Asia, some of them unexceptional, others less so. In China, for example, the government has tried to suppress an international meditation movement called Falun Gong, in which it perceives a political threat. And five years ago members of Aum Shinrikyo, an apocalyptic sect in Japan, attacked the Tokyo subways with the nerve gas sarin, killing 12 people and injuring 5,000.

Asked about his organization's place in the spectrum of new religious movements, Mr. Kiriyama described the association as strictly mainstream.

"Basically," he said, "Agon Buddhism is based on the direct and true words of the Buddha. It is as undiluted as possible. It has nothing to do with any kind of a cult."

As to why he chose a New York church to perform the association's first fire ritual in America, he said with a laugh, "Well, New York is the center of the world." He added that a religious ceremony ought to be held in a sacred space.

One of those invited to witness it is All Souls' pastor, the Rev. Forrester Church. "As a Unitarian church," the pastor said, "we try to tap into the genius of all faiths."

In the 19th century, All Souls played a role as a "religious crossroads" of New York, Mr. Church said, adding, "This is an opportunity for us to make it a religious crossroads for the world."

Text of New York Speech

A Conversation with One's Soul, A Battle with the Mind, and the Acquisition of Wisdom

November 4, 2000
Unitarian Church of All Souls, New York City

The Wisdom of the *Goma* Fire Ceremony

Ladies and Gentlemen, thank you all for coming.

And thank you Dr. Thellman for that kind introduction. I am Seiyu Kiriyama.

What you have just seen is a *goma* fire ritual.

In the time allowed, I'd like to explain a bit about the service.

I became a Buddhist practitioner in 1953, when I was 31 years old. I learned how to perform the fire ritual when I was 42. Since then I have performed it a countless number of times.

On average I perform this ceremony once a week and I have been doing it for 35 years, so I must have done it around seventeen hundred fifty times. At the very least, I've kindled fifteen hundred *goma* fires.

But even though I have done it so many times before, this is the first time I have ever performed a *goma* service like this one outside of Japan. I once kindled a *goma* fire in Taiwan, but that was an initiatory *goma*, not a wisdom *goma*.

Not that I haven't been offered the opportunity. I have traveled widely, giving lectures and dharma talks. Besides the United States, I've been to England, France, Italy, China, India, Sri Lanka, and Thailand, among many others. I have received numerous requests to perform this version of the ceremony. But I never

Kiriyama Kancho, against the backdrop of flames rising to the heavens from huge outdoor pyres, performs a blessing invoking good fortune.

Photographs by Kengo Tarumi

Agon Shu's Star Festival "The Great Shinto-Buddhist Fire Offering." White smoke billows forth and flames arise from the two *goma* pyres filled with millions of prayer sticks that record the thoughts and aspirations of the participants.

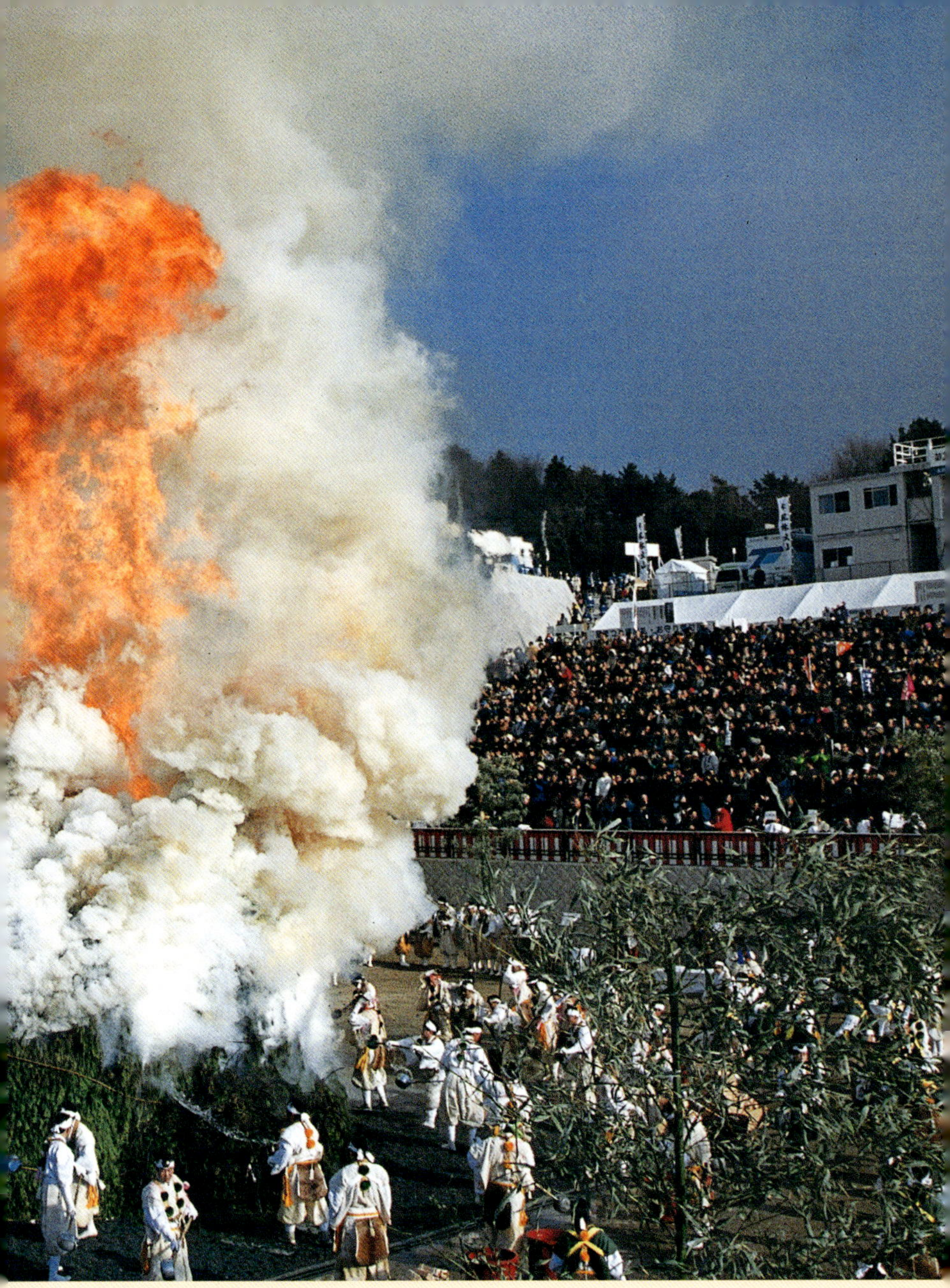

Frontal view of Agon Shu's main temple, Shakazan Daibodaiji. (Yamashina, Kyoto)

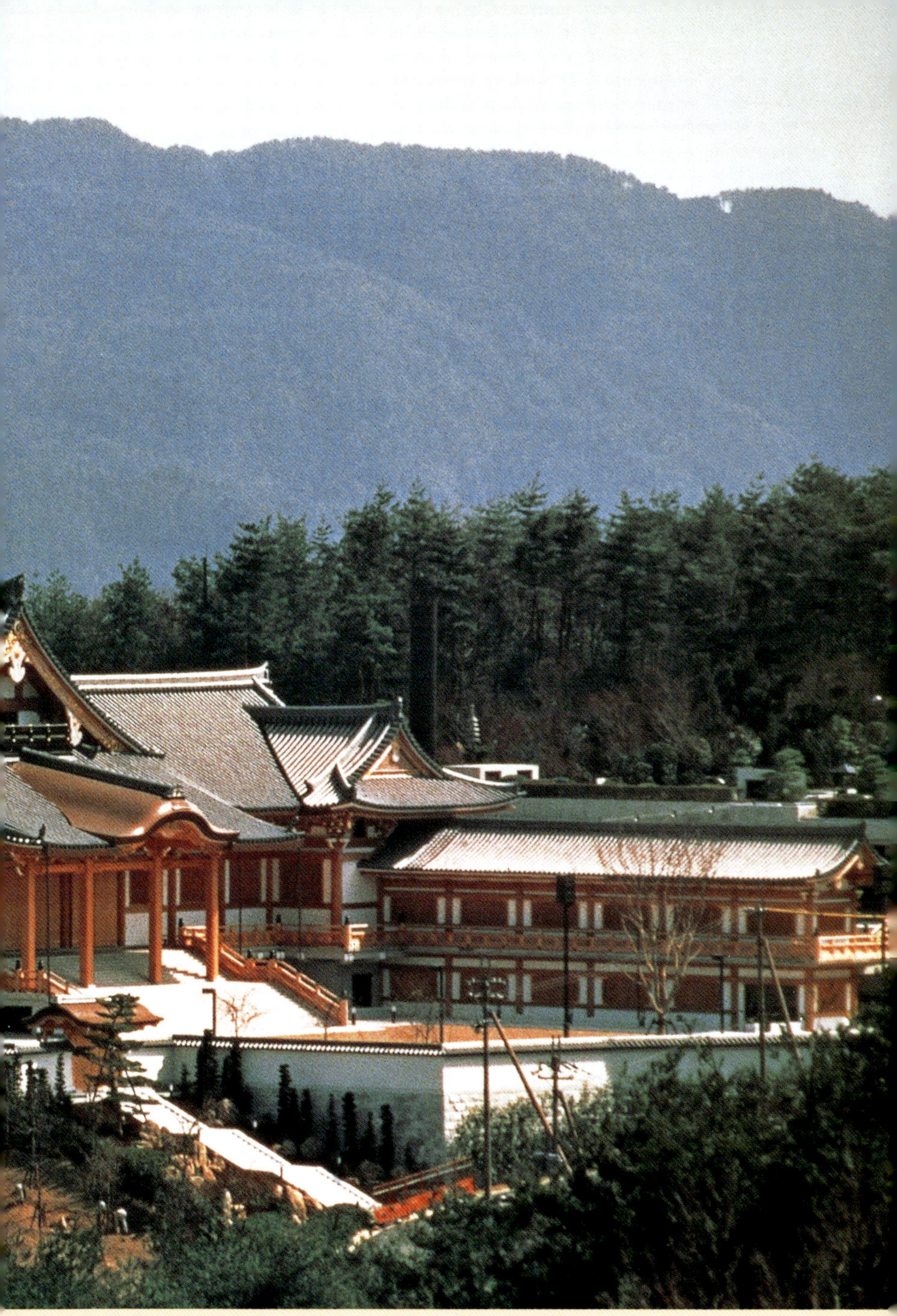

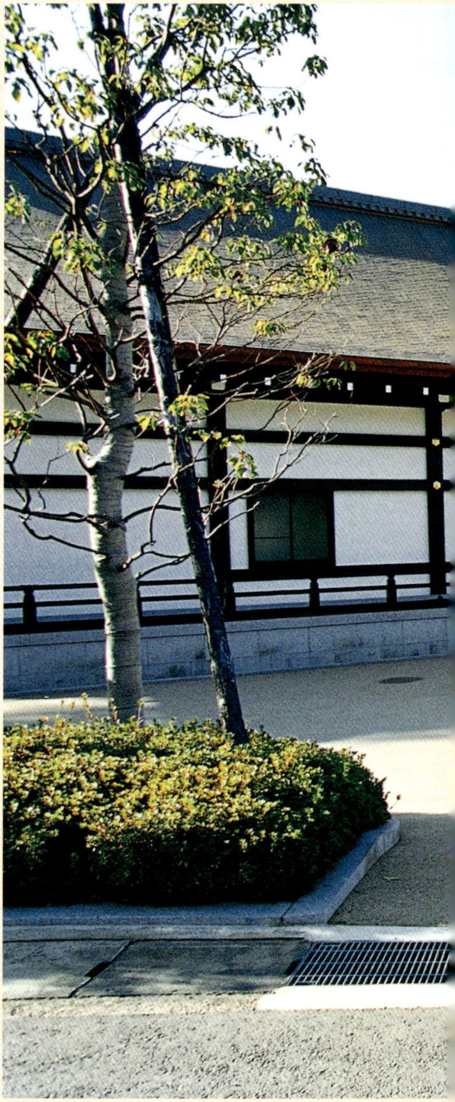

Frontal view of Agon Shu's spiritual training center, a facility for the practices that lead to the attainment of Nirvana.

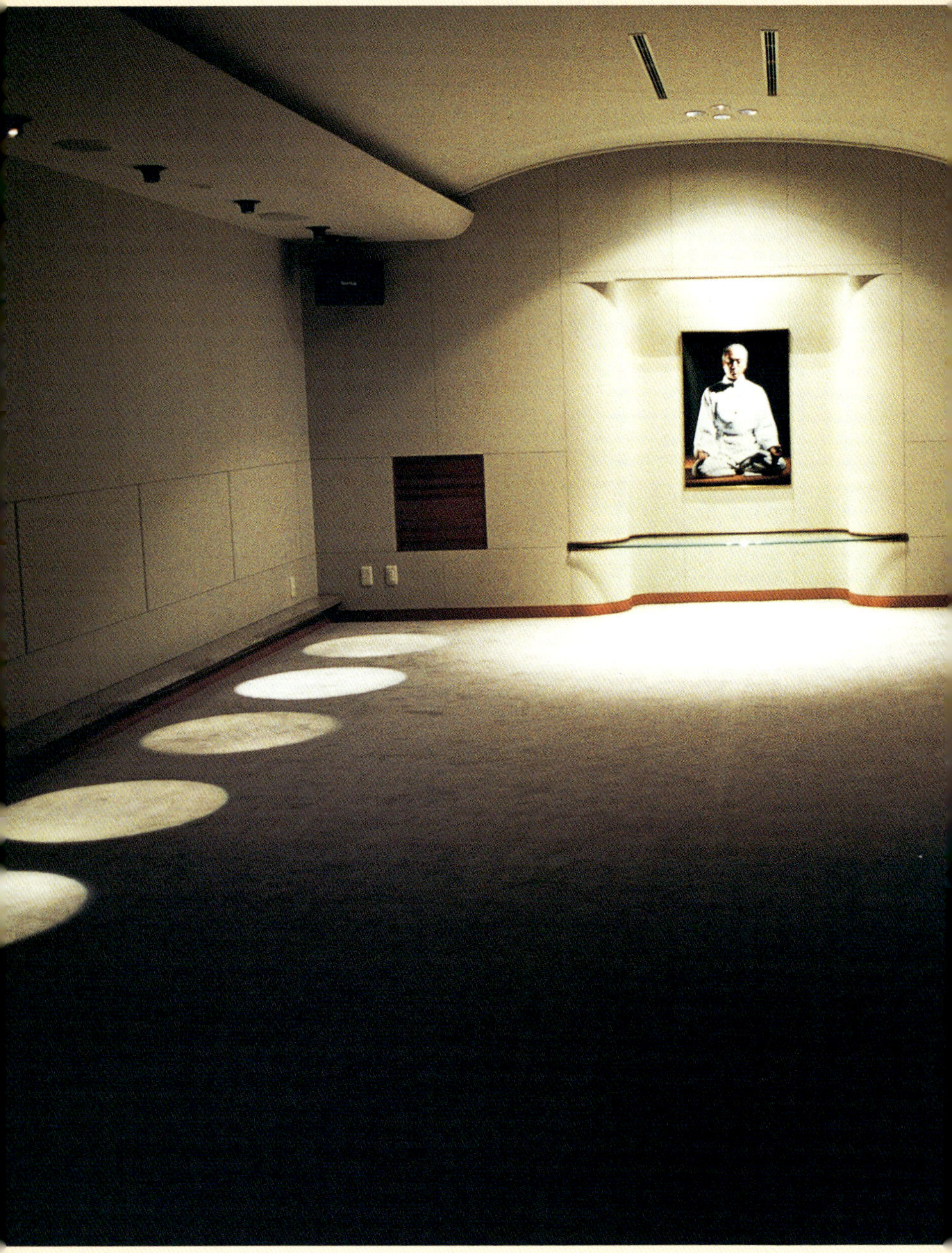

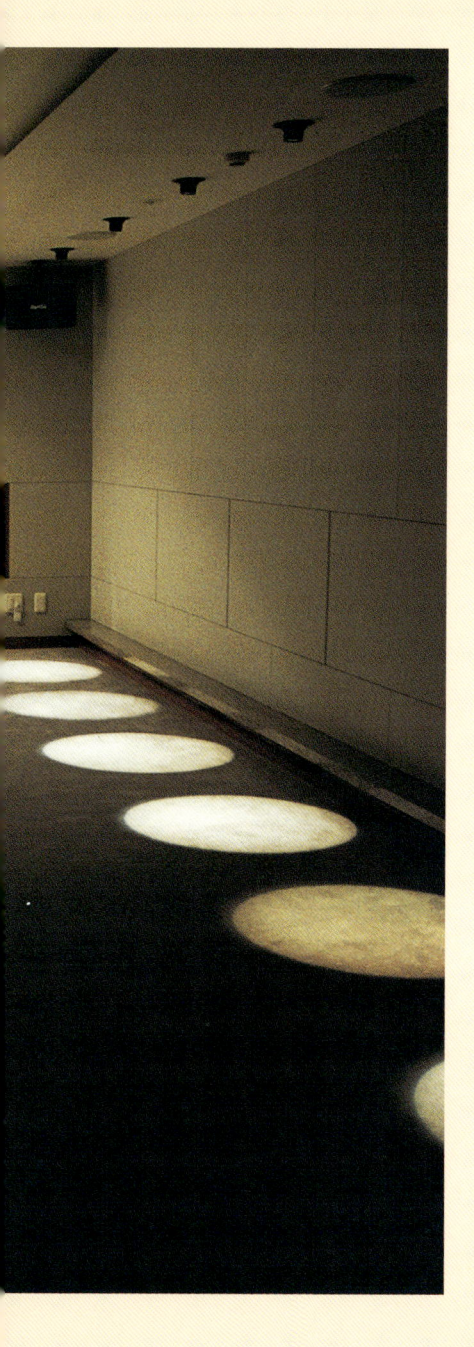

Meditation hall inside Agon Shu's spiritual training center.

Kiriyama Kancho performing a mudra under the *"Ryujin"* waterfall, designed for waterfall practice, at the training center.

"*Ryujin*" *goma* chamber, designed for the practice of the *goma* ceremony, at the training center.

Aerial view of Agon Shu's large compound that contains its main temple Shakazan Daibodaiji, the spiritual training center, and the site of the Star Festival.

agreed before.

Why is that?

It is because I have always felt that the first time I performed this kind of *goma* service outside of Japan it should happen in New York City.

New York is the information center of the world. I wanted to introduce Agon Buddhism's *goma* ritual to the world community from here.

As I will explain, this is because I believe the *goma* ritual contains vital information that people right now need to know.

But first, I must tell you what a joy it is to have actualized my dream here today.

Many people have contributed to the actualization of this event. Let me take this opportunity to offer my warmest gratitude to all the people behind the scenes who helped to make it possible. And thank you all for having made the effort to come here today. I am so grateful for your participation.

Let me talk about the three distinctive characteristics of the *goma* ritual as performed in Agon Shu.

The first of these is that the *goma* ritual is a "conversation with one's soul."

I believe that people cannot live the true life of a human being without having "a conversation with one's soul."

This is not the place for me to go into a detailed explanation and definition of what we mean by the word "soul."

For now, let me suggest that we human beings are more than a result of the interaction of our genetic DNA and the environment. Each of us has within ourselves a primary motivating energy that causes us to function as a living, individual human being. Whatever we call it, we know there is this something. For the sake of discussion, let us agree to refer to this as the soul.

I believe that the soul is something different than the spirit or the mind. I think it resides beyond the deepest layer of our consciousness, and that it is the fundamental mover of these other two. A unique quality of the soul is its purity.

The soul is rooted in universal consciousness. Its purity compels the soul to live an immaculate life. In contrast, the spirit and the mind face the enormous challenge of having to adapt to society (to the environment). This process sometimes distorts and represses the essential directives of the soul. The mind and the spirit become utilitarian. They learn expediency.

Thus, the mind and the spirit can become contaminated whereas the soul cannot. The purity of the soul is taintless.

This is why we must stay in conversation with the soul if we hope to be honest with ourselves and live a true life.

So how do we go about doing this?

How do we open the door to the soul, if the door

is located somewhere beyond the deepest layers of our consciousness?

We do it through harmony with universal consciousness.

The poet of psychoanalysis, Gaston Bachelard, has coined the term "Prometheus Complex" in *The Psychoanalysis of Fire*. He says:

> This is the true basis for the respect shown to flame: if the child brings his hand close to the fire his father raps over the knuckles with a ruler. Fire, then, can strike without having to burn. Whether this fire be flame or heat, lamp or stove, the parents' vigilance is the same. Thus fire is initially the object of a general prohibition; hence this conclusion: the social interdiction is our first general knowledge of fire. What we first learn about fire is that we must not touch it. As the child grows up, the prohibitions become intellectual rather than physical; the blow of the ruler is replaced by the angry voice; the angry voice by the recital of the dangers of fire, by the legends concerning fire from heaven. Thus the natural phenomenon is rapidly mixed in with complex and confused items of social experience which leave little room for the acquiring of an unprejudiced knowledge.

For Bachelard, fire clearly represents the conflict and internalized prohibitions that occur when a father reprimands a son in order to prevent him from getting burned.

He names this the "Prometheus Complex" after the Greek myth in which Prometheus steals fire from the gods to give to mankind and is severely punished by the king of the gods, Zeus.

My perception of fire is very different. Mine goes back to a much earlier age, all the way back to pre-historic times.

Fire is what separated man from the beasts. Fire gave man the impetus to form himself into social groups. It is what awakened the human being to spirituality.

Fire changed not only our way of life but the structure of our minds as well.

Fire leaves an indelibly vivid image in the unconscious. It is as if the flames perceived in the past continue to burn in the depths of our unconscious mind, remaining as long as consciousness and memory exist.

The fire that is burning deep in our consciousness is an excellent clue for discovering the door to our soul.

To the pre-historic people who had to live through the ice ages, fire was the mother; it was the father. Imagine them huddled inside ice-encrusted caves, their single hope for survival the fires burning in front of their eyes. The memory of this reality became deeply embedded in the human soul.

When you meditate as a *goma* practitioner in front of a quietly burning fire in a darkened chamber and you achieve ever-deepening stages of contemplation, these images appear again. You see the fire flickering in the cave, casting its long shadows against the walls. You hear the wind howling in the vast expanses of the wilderness punctuated by the roars of gigantic, unnamed beasts.

And then, quietly, as you go deeper, the door to the soul opens. And now you are able to begin a conversation with your soul.

The second distinctive characteristic of the *goma* ritual as practiced in Agon Shu is that it is "a battle with the mind."

After you have a deep quiet conversation with the soul, you begin to do serious battle with the mind, a battle of intelligence. In the same way that physical combat serves to train the body, this mental struggle acts to discipline and tone the intellect.

Before coming to New York, I sent ahead a message introducing the ritual. It contained the following comment:

> I particularly hope to have an impact on the young. If young people were as interested in attaining wisdom as they are in excelling at sports, the 21st century could witness the dawn

of a marvelous new world. I hope to demonstrate to young people that this specific form of meditation is, in fact, like a wonderfully compelling intellectual sport.

The *goma* ritual is obviously a religious ceremony. Those of you who read the message I sent ahead are probably wondering why I mentioned sports in a message about a religious subject. Here is why.

Agon Shu's fire ritual is like a martial art. In this way, it is even beyond a sport. You may be surprised at the analogy.

So whom am I fighting?

I am fighting with the mind.

Whose mind?

In the first place, my own. I am struggling with my mind as hard as I can. It requires all of my intelligence and ability.

I literally fight until the sparks fly.

There is a magnificence in the battle, just as there is in wrestling, or boxing, or *sumo*, and glory like in baseball, soccer, football, or rugby.

People who can see into the spiritual dimension watch the battle of the *goma* in awe.

My own mind, however, is not my only opponent. I also struggle with the minds of all those who have gone before me.

First there is the Buddha, who deserves our eternal respect. And then his great disciples.

And then the philosophers, starting with Socrates and Plato and moving on to Kant, Descartes, Hegel, Nietzsche, Jaspers, and Heidegger. They make formidable opponents. And then there are Confucius and Mencius.

There are hosts of other spiritual geniuses who are ready and waiting to engage in the contest: masters, heroes, and veterans of other contests.

An incalculable number of them. Shakespeare, Balzac, Tolstoi, Beethoven, Haydn, Chopin, Michelangelo, Picasso. Anyone you might want to fight with is there. However, it is not simply an intellectual battle. It is a battle of the spirit, of the mind.

How does one go about waging this battle?

It takes all the strength one has, thrusting and wrestling and twisting to gain advantage in one's struggle with these people.

Doesn't it sound like a really fun contest?

It doesn't matter if you win or lose. The joy and meaning is in the struggle, in making your mind sweat. The excitement feels good, like when you are invigorated by a really good workout.

Did you know that your mind has muscles too?

Now, of course, the mental battle that takes place during the *goma* ritual requires its own unique skills and techniques.

As in any sport or martial art, there are specific ways of training for the event and certain rules that must be followed. There is a protocol to the battle.

The techniques of the mental battle of the fire ritual are based on the method the Buddha taught known as *jobutsuho*, or "means of attaining Buddhahood." As the name indicates, this is the method whose practice and application will turn you into a Buddha. And it is the only one we have. If you decide that you want to be a Buddha, this is the path that will take you there. Accordingly, perfect mastery of this method guarantees that you will attain Buddhahood. This is something that the Buddha taught in the Agama Sutras. I based my spiritual battle techniques on the "means of attaining Buddhahood," and added some methods of my own to develop the system I use.

This system helps to build the kind of spirit that one needs to become a Buddha. A spirit that is tough, flexible, and wise.

In a word, what burns during the *goma* ritual is not firewood. It is the energy of my mind. A person's mind has vibrations, as do the flames of the *goma* fire. I send out waves of energy from my mind into the *goma* fire that resonate and amplify each other. As I direct my mental energy into the crackling fire, the energy of the fire acts to elevate my own. I continue to pour this elevated mental energy back into the fire and then transfer it back again into my own mind. The *goma* altar becomes a kind of crucible of mental energy. In an overstatement that may help to explain the concept, the altar becomes like a nuclear reactor of the mind.

I use the enormously transformed energy of my

mind to begin the grand battles with the spiritual titans that I now undertake.

There is one more distinctive characteristic of Agon Shu's *goma* ritual. This is the "acquisition of wisdom."

The *goma* ritual is one of the earth's oldest religious ceremonies. It is mentioned in the Vedas, the ancient Indian scriptures that were written about 3,000 years ago.

The word *goma* is the Sino-Japanese transliteration of the Sanskrit word *homa*. The *homa* is a religious rite that has been associated with Brahmanism since olden times and is one that is still practiced widely in India to this day.

The Brahmanic *homa* consisted of casting a votive offering into a fire, of placing it directly, as it were, into the hands of the fire god Agni, who sent it up to heaven. It was believed that as the flames ascended to heaven they reached the mouths of the gods who would then answer the prayers of the petitioner.

Buddhism incorporated the *homa* into its liturgy, adopting the form but largely changing the content of the ritual.

Buddhism systematized the *goma* into a ceremony that combined the secular invocation of good fortune with the higher attainment of Buddhist spiritual liberation.

In other words it infused a Brahmanic festival with Buddhist doctrine.

Specifically, it equated the *goma* fire with the wisdom of the Buddha.

That is, the *goma* fire was no longer seen as simple fire. Instead, it was seen as a direct representation of the Buddha's wisdom. The Buddha's wisdom fire possesses the ability to burn up human defilement and the power to bring about the realization of enlightenment.

In Brahmanism the fire ritual is merely a means of conveying votive offerings to the gods. In Buddhism, the ritual is a means, through the fire of the Buddha's wisdom, to attain enlightenment. This theory transforms the ritual into an expression of highest Buddhist doctrine.

After I became a Buddhist practitioner, I was very taken with esoteric Buddhism and began to study the *goma* ritual.

While seriously involved in the practice I began to have questions about the theory behind it.

I understood that the fire was supposed to be the Buddha's wisdom. And to that I had no objections. But I had trouble discovering the method, the means, for transforming the ordinary *goma* fire into that of the Buddha's wisdom. If one was simply to visualize in one's mind that the fire was the Buddha's wisdom, then the practice was nothing more than ideation. There had to be a way to actually change the fire into that of the Buddha's wisdom. If there wasn't, then it was just a plain old bonfire.

What was the method?

This was my question.

Unfortunately there is no time to go into detail here, but, in short, I wrestled with this problem for over ten years until I figured out a solution. In the end my search led me to the Agama Sutras.

Historically, the Agama Sutras were not taken seriously in Japan. They were relegated to the ranks of Hinayana scripture and, as such, deemed inferior and not worthy of attention. I believe that this was a huge mistake. In fact, as I found, the Agama Sutras are the only authentic records of the Buddha's teachings.

One of the reasons why the Agama Sutras are so precious is because they contain the teachings on the "means for attaining Buddhahood."

As I touched upon before, this is the method for turning oneself into a Buddha. I need to stress the word "method." It is not just a "teaching," a string of words that one needs to understand. It is a "method." It is something "to do."

The Mahayana sutras contain teachings about becoming a Buddha but they don't give instructions about how to actually do it. This method is found only in the Agama Sutras. Nowhere else. When I discovered this I established Agon Shu as a way of sharing what I'd found with others.

The method for attaining Buddhahood recorded in the Agama Sutras is known as the "7 Systems and 37 Practices Conducive to Enlightenment." It is comprised of 7 subjects divided into 37 kinds of spiritual practices.

I refer to it as the "7 Systems and 37 Curricula for the Attainment of Sacred Wisdom."

In short, this method leads to the perfect embodiment of the Buddha's wisdom. And if someone has attained wisdom identical to that of the Buddha, then hasn't he or she become a Buddha in his or her own right?

I myself have practiced this method. I have not yet mastered it perfectly, but I have the confidence to say that I am almost there.

In conclusion, I'd like to say that I was able to devise my version of the *goma* fire ritual by means of the "method of attaining Buddhahood." I was able to succeed because of it.

If you perform the *goma* ritual through this method the fire will definitely be the fire of the Buddha's wisdom. And if you perform this *goma*, I can assure you that you will realize the wisdom of the Buddha, safely and reliably.

I am willing to teach the *goma* of the Buddha's wisdom to anyone who wishes to learn it. That is why I came to New York.

Can you imagine how wonderful this world would become if we saw the emergence of more and more sagacious men and women who possessed the wisdom of the Buddha?

I think that wisdom is the consummate thing. I think it is supreme. I also believe that, right now, wisdom is more important for the human race than anything else.

Compassion and love are also critical attributes. We must have them in this world. But they don't necessarily include wisdom, whereas the attainment of the highest wisdom always encompasses love and compassion.

Again, let me repeat. Compassion and love are completely necessary in this world. But they don't necessarily include wisdom, whereas the attainment of the highest wisdom always encompasses love and compassion.

The road is open to you. Every one of you can become a Buddha. You! And you! And you!

Thank you very much for your kind attention.

Towards Attaining semi-Nirvana

True Happiness Is Obtained through Wisdom

Japanese Mahayana Buddhism teaches that salvation comes through compassion. Christianity teaches that it comes through love. In contrast, Agon Buddhism (Buddhism based on the Agama Sutras) teaches that salvation comes through wisdom. It believes that the most important thing for human beings, therefore, is not compassion or love but wisdom. Because when one obtains wisdom the compassion and love that one needs arise spontaneously within one's being. And, furthermore, people cannot be saved through compassion alone.

Man requires wisdom. When human beings become wise they can achieve true happiness by themselves. The happiness that one receives through the compassion of others is not real happiness. Wouldn't you agree? Happiness is something we need to find by ourselves. But how do we go about it?

Wisdom is the only way.

True happiness cannot be achieved through receiving love or compassion from someone else. It can only be obtained through burnishing one's own wisdom and one's own power.

Why do human beings hurt each other? Why do we kill each other? Why do we take things from each other?

Because of ignorance. As one reaps what one sows, ignorant behavior produces unhappiness. Everyone knows that murder, assault, and deprivation do not lead to happiness. Yet they continue unabated. Why? Because of human ignorance.

Any given country may be home to a multitude of intelligent people yet still decide to go to war, killing scores of people in the process. How does this happen?

One of the essential qualities of the human being is ignorance. That is why the emergence of one or two truly wise people has the potential to transform the world. Wisdom is what we lack. Its acquisition is what can bring about true change.

This is not merely my own supposition. It is an idea that Shakyamuni Buddha taught. He did not speak of it in such a direct fashion, but in studying his teachings we see clearly that it is what he meant. And that is why he left very specific instructions on how to go about attaining true wisdom. He left a method.

This method is known as the "7 Systems and 37 Practices Conducive to Enlightenment." Anyone who engages in the spiritual practice of this method will become a wisdom being. At the very least, one is sure to become wiser than one was before. One can always tell who has practiced this method and who hasn't because the difference between them is so apparent. This is not to say that love and compassion are irrelevant. They are necessary too, of course. But the attainment of true wisdom brings about a consequent, natural awakening of love and compassion. So we must seek wisdom. Shakyamuni Buddha asserts this to be so and so does Agon Buddhism.

After deep contemplation, I arrived at the conclusion that the doctrinal theory based on the "7 Systems and 37 Practices Conducive to Enlightenment" that Shakyamuni Buddha taught is the only true way to attain salvation.

It will be interesting to see what happens. I suspect that in the 21st century all the major religions of the world will move closer to the ideas expressed in the Buddhism of the Agama Sutras. If they don't, we might not make it. These ideas are vital to the continuation of our planet. I am convinced of it. And that is why I have devoted my life to their propagation.

Establishment of a Training Center

How do we put this theory into practice?
We work towards the attainment of semi-Nirvana.
And what is semi-Nirvana?
Semi-Nirvana is the ideal state of body and mind that a human being attains through the performance of spiritual practice.

More specifically, semi-Nirvana is a state in which

one's spirit, emotions, intelligence, and physical body have been made as efficacious and reliable as possible so that one can fully utilize all the power at one's disposal.

It is the state that precedes the stage of complete Nirvana. That is why it is called semi-Nirvana.

One obtains the preliminary state of semi-Nirvana through the performance of the "7 Systems and 37 Practices Conducive to Enlightenment."

When I use the term "spiritual practice" I am referring specifically to the spiritual discipline of the "7 Systems and 37 Practices Conducive to Enlightenment." Through this discipline, a practitioner achieves the optimal state of mental and physical conditioning possible for him or for her.

Over the last few decades I have wanted to establish an ideal environment in which to transmit these teachings. One of the ways I have tried to do this is to hold relatively short retreats, from two to five days, during which the participants engage in intense study and practice. But this is not enough time for the students to gain mastery over any given teaching. It is only a partial solution, a way to introduce them to teachings and disciplines that they will hopefully be able to pursue more thoroughly in the future. The short retreat format works well for this purpose.

But in order to reap the true benefits of spiritual practice one must perform it consistently over an extended period of time.

And so Agon Shu decided to build a training center where practitioners could carry out more intensive long-term practice. We have created a waterfall specifically for waterfall asceticism and a fire ritual chamber specifically for the practice of the *goma* ceremony. Designed to fully meet the needs of the spiritual practitioner, I know of no other *dojo* in the world that compares to it.

Gaining proficiency at any trivial pursuit takes a certain amount of effort and dedication. Imagine how much truer this must be for something as serious as the spiritual practices of the Buddhist path. I myself spent over ten years in wholehearted and exclusive devotion to Buddhist practice. During that time, day and night, I thought of nothing else besides religious matters, besides Buddhism. It was only when I completed this initial stage of my journey that I became aware of the doctrines of Agon Buddhism.

Ordinary human effort brings ordinary human results. This is true even if one possesses some degree of genius. I may have had a certain aptitude for the spiritual path but I was only able to actualize my propensity through concentrated and sustained effort. So the issue becomes not the aptitude for the path but the aptitude for the exertion required to pursue it, for the sustained effort needed to succeed. One cannot accomplish something by doing nothing. That sort of aptitude doesn't exist.

There are people who are unable to exert themselves. However hard they try they just can't, no matter how much they may want to. There may be a physical cause for their inability. Maybe they are so weak that they lack endurance. When we look at it this way, health itself is a kind of aptitude. Having a healthy body with strong internal organs is a prerequisite faculty. It is almost impossible to endure the rigors of intensive spiritual practice if one is not well, even if one is enthusiastic and determined. So one must do one's best to become as healthy as possible so that one possesses the amount of energy that the spiritual path requires.

I believe that everyone has aptitude. But not everyone is able to strive to attain a certain goal. I sometimes encounter a person who I know would benefit greatly from a period of diligent spiritual practice, for say a year. But if the person is inconstant and flighty, he or she may well quit after a month, unable to continue. But, the practice itself would have had the power to correct the underlying character flaw.

I am someone who became well aware of the flaws in my own character. In order to correct them, I wrote them down in a notebook and made myself look over the list a number of times every day during the time I was undergoing spiritual training so that I could check up on how I was doing. I watched as each one of the deficiencies improved over time. It took about three years before they had practically disappeared, giving truth to the old saying "Perseverance will win in the end."

Begin by Healing Mind and Body

Returning to the discussion of semi-Nirvana, one obtains three qualities as a result of this spiritual practice. They are:
TOUGHNESS
WISENESS
HAPPINESS

"Toughness" means strength of mind and body, "wiseness" means wisdom, and "happiness" means the overall sense of happiness that surrounds one as one continues on with the practice.

As you can see in the diagram, I have divided practice into five steps. But this is just one manner in which the variety of spiritual practices can be organized. Also, not all the different spiritual practices have been included here.

Strictly speaking, the content of one person's practice is different from that of another. This system of spiritual practice is not universal but must be tailored to the individual practitioner. However, these steps are meant to provide us with a useful standard for comparison. Also, certain practices have been omitted on

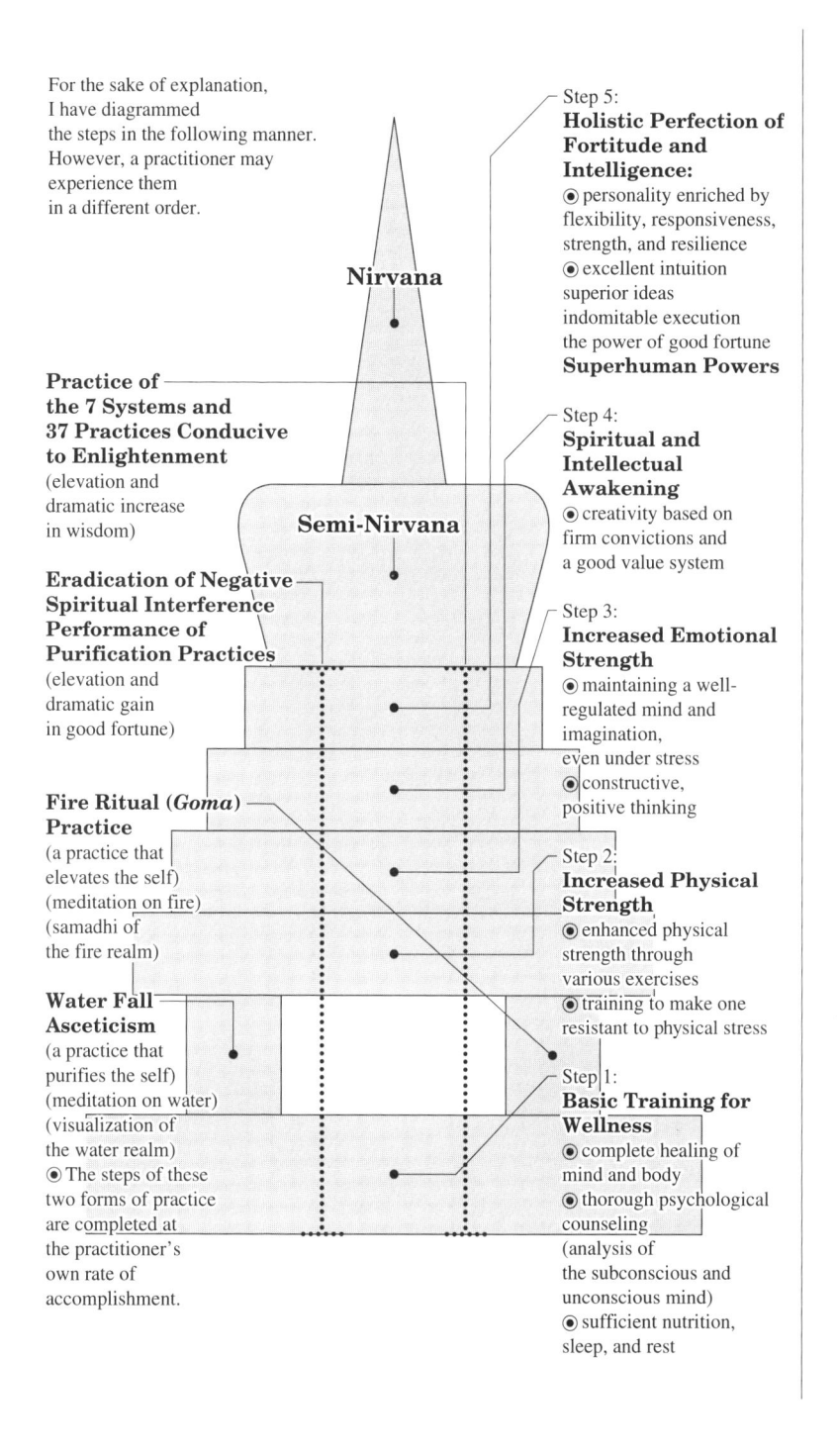

For the sake of explanation, I have diagrammed the steps in the following manner. However, a practitioner may experience them in a different order.

Nirvana

Semi-Nirvana

Practice of the 7 Systems and 37 Practices Conducive to Enlightenment
(elevation and dramatic increase in wisdom)

Eradication of Negative Spiritual Interference
Performance of Purification Practices
(elevation and dramatic gain in good fortune)

Fire Ritual (*Goma*) Practice
(a practice that elevates the self)
(meditation on fire)
(samadhi of the fire realm)

Water Fall Asceticism
(a practice that purifies the self)
(meditation on water)
(visualization of the water realm)
⊙ The steps of these two forms of practice are completed at the practitioner's own rate of accomplishment.

Step 5:
Holistic Perfection of Fortitude and Intelligence:
⊙ personality enriched by flexibility, responsiveness, strength, and resilience
⊙ excellent intuition
superior ideas
indomitable execution
the power of good fortune
Superhuman Powers

Step 4:
Spiritual and Intellectual Awakening
⊙ creativity based on firm convictions and a good value system

Step 3:
Increased Emotional Strength
⊙ maintaining a well-regulated mind and imagination, even under stress
⊙ constructive, positive thinking

Step 2:
Increased Physical Strength
⊙ enhanced physical strength through various exercises
⊙ training to make one resistant to physical stress

Step 1:
Basic Training for Wellness
⊙ complete healing of mind and body
⊙ thorough psychological counseling
(analysis of the subconscious and unconscious mind)
⊙ sufficient nutrition, sleep, and rest

purpose because of their esoteric nature.

Step 1 is "Basic Training for Wellness." Every practitioner brings with him or her certain sets of physical and psychological problems. We first begin by remedying them. In concrete terms, we effect a "complete healing of mind and body," a "thorough counseling," and "sufficient nutrition, sleep, and rest."

First, the complete healing of mind and body. I doubt if there is anyone who is free from psychological wounds. Or physical wounds for that matter, where wounds are taken to mean weaknesses. For example, a person may have a weak liver or a weak stomach or a weak heart.

Agon Shu's spiritual practices help one become a kind of superbeing whose capabilities expand beyond the ordinary. One becomes capable of meeting the vicissitudes of life and making one's way in the world with ease.

The first step in attaining this sort of capability is to bring about the complete healing of mind and body. We try to resolve any mental difficulties that a person may be experiencing through a program of thorough counseling. After identifying areas of stress and difficulty, we work to address and relieve them.

Some might claim that they have no mental conflict and they aren't under any stress, but I beg to differ. No one is stressfree. I am not only referring to the kind of stress that affects surface consciousness. That kind of stress is relatively easy to identify and deal with. I am also talking about the kind of stress that occurs in the deeper layers of consciousness, in the subconscious and the unconscious. This kind of stress is much more problematic.

The stress lodged in the subconscious or the unconscious is called repressed consciousness. I classify repression into two types that I refer to as the Freudian type and the Szondian type.

The repressed consciousness (stress) at the base of the subconscious and the unconscious is strongly connected to negative spiritual interference. As such, it falls outside the realm of medicine. Medical doctors and psychologists are therefore hard pressed to eliminate it. Its removal requires the kind of spiritual skill and powers of Buddhist attainment that Agon Shu possesses. These powers are capable of eliminating the kind of spiritually connected repression that medicine and psychology cannot.

Mental problems may arise that appear to be unconnected to the spiritual realm. The human mind is a truly complicated affair, and spiritual interference may insidiously impact surface consciousness as disturbances and confusion that may result in an abnormality of that layer of mind as well. These also must be corrected.

This resolution is connected to Step 3, "Increased Emotional Strength." The complete resolution of stress doesn't happen overnight, but requires diligence and patience over an extended period of time.

Proper Nutrition Supports Spiritual Practice

The third item of Step 1 is "sufficient nutrition, sleep, and rest." This is key. The majority of people today are not getting enough nutrition, sleep, or rest.

This produces a constant source of low-level anxiety that is stressful for surface consciousness.

"Sufficient nutrition" does not mean that one needs to eat luxurious and elaborate meals. It means one needs to eat food that is full of nutrients, something fewer and fewer people are doing in the fast-paced modern world. There was an interesting article in the morning edition of the *Asahi Newspaper* last February 5. The headline read "Consumption of Junk Food Causes Nutritional Deficiency in Junior High Students. Experts Find Link to Behavioral Problems." The article discussed the relationship between nutrition and adolescent unruliness and delinquency. It suggested that there are definite links between nutritional deficiencies due to eating patterns and the increase in delinquency and violence among teenagers we see today.

An examination of what young people are actually eating reveals appalling dietary patterns. A typical breakfast is one piece of white bread and some milk. Some don't even drink the milk. They slather some butter or jam on a piece of bread, gobble it down, then head out the door. Some of them don't even eat that much. Lunch is a hamburger or some instant noodles. They eat snacks and drink juice and never really sit down to a proper meal. They are only eating to fill their stomachs. No wonder they become unruly and listless.

Again, eating smart doesn't have to be luxurious or expensive. A good meal is one that is packed with balanced nutrition. It doesn't have to be costly.

Like most traditional home cooking. In Japan, a traditional meal might consist of rice cooked with barley, a plate of dried sardines, miso soup made with seaweed, and steamed greens like spinach. This is the kind of food that "mother used to make," though this mother may have lived fifty years ago rather than anytime in recent memory.

The animal protein in a meal like this comes from fish. Or one might eat a moderate amount of meat. In either event, I believe that the kind of nutrition contained in a meal like this, if eaten regularly, could cut adolescent behavioral problems in half. Or possibly even by 60%.

In our training center we teach how to eat properly. We also demonstrate ways to fix nutritious meals in much less time than the hour or two required to prepare traditional ones so that people can do it themselves when they go home.

Sleep is also important. People who are anxious and under great stress do not sleep well. They stay in a light sleep all night long without entering the deeper stages of slumber. They cannot recuperate from their exhaustion. Or they stay up until one or two in the morning. Both kinds of people wake up feeling tired and groggy.

We correct these sleep deficiencies. Because nutritional deficiency and lack of exercise are leading causes of the inability to sleep, we need to correct these two imbalances as well. Accordingly, we teach participants appropriate ways to exercise.

Next comes rest. I make this a separate category because contemporary men and women really don't know how to rest. Watching TV is not resting. One doesn't need a long time to give one's mind and body pause. A five-minute rest, say, in the yoga posture known as "the corpse" can be enough.

Once during summer retreat I taught this posture to a group of about 200 people. They all fell into a deep sleep. I thought I'd let them sleep for about 10 minutes but they were sleeping so soundly I didn't have the heart to wake them. Not one person opened their eyes before I finally woke them up 30 minutes later. It made me realize how tired people are today. People don't know the meaning of real rest or sleep.

And so we teach it to them.

Strengthening Mind and Body

Step 2 is training for "Increased Physical Strength." It is comprised of "various exercises to enhance physical strength" and "training to make one resistant to physical stress." At this stage we introduce the practice of waterfall asceticism to those who are ready for it. In my experience, waterfall asceticism has been the single most effective means of achieving these aims. It strengthens both mind and body.

Though wonderfully effective, it is also extremely demanding. We therefore require a doctor's examination before we allow anyone to do it. It is too dangerous for anyone who has heart problems, for example. People need to achieve the basic level of physical strength indicated in Step 1 before they are ready to undertake the practice of waterfall asceticism.

Because we have practitioners of all ages and shapes and sizes, I am thinking about devising a system whereby we can actually adjust the degree of water temperature and pressure to individual circumstance.

Waterfall asceticism is also brilliant in increasing one's ability to resist stress. It enables one to rise above all the small things and makes one impervious to petty irritations. It also helps one to sleep well at night. I encourage the practitioner to continue the practice until these basic goals have been met.

Step 3 is training for "Increased Emotional Strength." It enables one to "maintain a well-regulated mind and imagination, even under stress" and "constructive, positive thinking."

Emotional strength does not mean stubbornness. Of all the shortcomings a person can have, stubbornness and obstinacy are some of the worst. They make it impossible to listen to the advice of other people and induce the problematic belief that one is always right.

It is important that emotional strength have a spirit of flexibility.

These practices enable one to maintain a mental life that, even when under stress, is characterized by an imagination based on orderly, positive thought.

A person's life will vary dramatically depending on whether he or she is a positive or negative thinker. Which predicts the happier future? Positive thinking, of course.

Step 4 is "Spiritual and Intellectual Awakening." These practices engender creativity based on firm convictions and a good value system. Step 5 is "Holistic Perfection of Fortitude and Intelligence." The practices contained in Step 5 produce a "personality enriched by flexibility, responsiveness, strength, and resilience. One is no longer stressed. In fact, as a result of the practices of mental enhancement, stress itself becomes a positive stimulus to the development of excellent intuition, superior ideas, indomitable execution, and the power of good fortune."

The "7 Systems and 37 Practices Conducive to Enlightenment" are practices of mental enhancement. I haven't written about it here, but one of the divisions of this method specifically deals with increasing mental ability. In these practices, even stress is turned into a positive force that is used to beneficial effect.

Sakrdagamin: Intellectual Completion

In Step 5 there is intellectual completion at the same time that there is accomplishment of the practices to enhance mental power included in the "7 Systems and 37 Practices Conducive to Enlightenment." Thus one completes a certain stage of spiritual practice.

Beyond Step 5 are the stages of spiritual completion in which one eventually reaches the level of the *anagamin*, a being who has attained spiritual completion. This is very difficult to achieve.

There are 4 stages that lead to liberation. These are:

Srotapanna—a wise person who has destroyed and purified all the taints
Sakrdagamin—a wise person who has been elevated
Anagamin—a saint who leaps dimensions

Arhat—a perfect Buddha

Semi-Nirvana is almost the realm of *sakrdagamin*. The 's' of semi-Nirvana also stands for the 's' in *sakrdagamin*. Some practitioners may reach the stage of *anagamin*, a state that is very close to Nirvana and from which the practitioner may soon move on to arhatship, but this is an extremely difficult achievement. May all attain its accomplishment, but, in the meantime, one is sure to reach the stage of *sakrdagamin* if one undertakes the practices noted above.

Agon Shu's doctrinal theory is actualized through the spiritual practices that lead to semi-Nirvana. Briefly, this is a basic outline of the method of spiritual practices employed by Agon Shu.

About the Author

Seiyu Kiriyama
Founder of Agon Shu Buddhist Association;
Professor Emeritus of Peking University;
Professor Emeritus of Zhongshan University;
Professor Emeritus of The National Buddhist Seminary of China (Buddhist College);
Member of the Board of Directors, University of San Francisco;
Professor Emeritus and Honorary Doctor of Philosophy, National University of Mongolia;
Visiting Professor and Honorary Dean of the Nyingmapa Tibetan Buddhist College;
Honorary Archbishop of the Siam Sect of Sri Lankan Buddhism;
Title of the Highest Rank of the Clergy of Myanmar Buddhism;
Director of the Chinese International Qigong Research Center (Beijing);
Honorary Member of the Dutch Treat Club, New York;
Honorary Eighth Rank, Japanese Go Association.

Author of 50 books,
including "Agon Buddhism as the Source of 'Shamatha (Tranquillity) and Vipashyanā (Insight)'," "The Varieties of Karma," "21st Century: The Age of *Sophia*," and "You Have Been Here Before: Reincarnation," and the soon-to-be-released "The Secret of Miracles" and "The Practitioner's Guide to Agon Buddhism."

AGON SHU OFFICE ADDRESSES

Kanto Main Office
Agon Shu Kanto Betsuin
4-14-15 Mita, Minato-ku,Tokyo
108-8318, JAPAN
81-3-3769-1931

Kansai Main Office
Agon Shu Kansai So-honbu
Jingumichi Agaru Sanjodori
Higashiyama-ku, Kyoto City
605-0031, JAPAN
81-75-761-1141

Hawaii Branch Office
Agon Mission of Hawaii
The Tradewinds B-1-C
1720 Ala Moana Blvd.
Honolulu, Hawaii, 96815, U.S.A.
1-808-949-4652

California Branch Office
Agon Shu U.S.A.
15418 S.Western Ave.,
Gardena,California, 90247,U.S.A.
1-310-768-8068

New York Branch Office
Agon Shu Buddhist Association
416 East 59th St., New York,
N.Y. 10022, U.S.A.
1-212-754-0757

Brazil Branch Office
Associacao Budista Agon Shu Do Brasil
Rua Dr.Getulio Vargas Filho,
No.131-Jabaquara
Cep.04318 Sao Paulo-Sp, BRASIL
55-11-5011-2102

Europe Branch Office
Agon Shu UK
3 Queen Square, London WC1N 3AU,
England, UK
44-20-7278-1988

Canada Branch Office
Agon Shu Canada Buddhist
Association
1255 Yonge St., Suite 302,
Toronto,Ontario M4T1W6,
CANADA
1-416-922-1272

Taipei Main Office
Agon Shu Taipei Honbu
2F NO.30 Lane 25 Dong Shan Rd.
Shihlin,Taipei,TAIWAN
886-2-2874-0660

Kaohsiung Branch Office
Agon Shu Takao Shibu
5F.NO.201 Sui Yuen RD.
Kaohsiung,TAIWAN ROC
886-7-3808909

Main Temple
Shakazan Daibodai-ji
Omine-cho,Yamashina-ku,
Kyoto City 607-8471, JAPAN

THE WISDOM OF THE *GOMA* FIRE CEREMONY

ニューヨークより世界に向けて発信す【英語版】

2001年5月10日　第1版第1刷発行

著　者……桐山靖雄
　　　　　Ⓒ 2001 by Seiyu Kiriyama
訳　者……ランディ・ブラウン
発行者……森眞智子
発行所……株式会社平河出版社
　　　　　〒108-0073東京都港区三田3-1-5
　　　　　TEL.03(3454)4885
　　　　　FAX.03(5484)1660
　　　　　振替00110-4-117324
装　幀……谷村彰彦
印刷所……日本写真印刷株式会社
用紙店……中庄株式会社

落丁・乱丁本はお取り替えいたします。
Printed in Japan 2001
ISBN4-89203-313-8　C0015
本書の引用は自由ですが、必ず著者の承諾を得ること。

Published in conjunction with the author's lecture on 4 November 2000 in New York.

You Have Been Here Before:
Reincarnation

by Seiyu Kiriyama

Translated by Rande Brown

Does reincarnation really exist?
Why do you reincarnate?
What is it that actually reincarnates?
With his highly developed psychic clairvoyance and wisdom,
the author clarifies the world after death and the secrets of reincarnation.

● 1000 yen

Published in conjunction with the author's invited visit on 8 June 2000 to the School of Oriental and African Studies, University of London.

Let's give some thought to wisdom!

21st Century: The Age of *Sophia*

The Wisdom of Greek Philosophy and the Wisdom of the Buddha

by Seiyu Kiriyama

Translated by Rande Brown

Wisdom is the very essence of life. Without wisdom nations, societies, businesses and people all go to ruin. This book compares the wisdom of Greek philosophy and the wisdom of Gotama Buddha, the two ultimate expressions of human wisdom, and explains how to cultivate wisdom.

● 900 yen

Agon Buddhism as the Source of "Shamatha (Tranquillity) and Vipashyanā (Insight)"

The Two Enigmas of T'ien-t'ai Master Chih-i

by Seiyu Kiriyama

Translated by Rande Brown

This book presents the text of a lecture given by the author at Peking University, China, on 9 November 1998. The Buddha sought "nirvana," T'ien-t'ai Master Chih-i sought "emptiness," and Ch'an(orZen)sought "nothingness," and in this epoch-makingbook the author discusses these three currents chiefly with reference to Chih-i's *Mo-ho chih-kuan(The Great Shamatha and Vipashyanā)*. In addition, it also includes the text of the author's lecture"Agon Buddhism as Sozialwissenschaft: Introduction," delivered at Zhongshan University on 4 December 1997.

● 1300 yen